Blessings

Verses of Grace
and Faith

R. A. Gilmore

ISBN: 979-8-9872766-2-4

Table of Contents

Preface

God has been, and is, my inspiration for the writing of poems. He provides the impetus and the ideas for the poems. From my perspective, when the Spirit moves, I write. Letting God lead in this process has been very rewarding and the results are pleasing to the eye, and to the ear. While I perform the writing, I'm more and more convinced that the true author of the poems is God.

I'm thankful the Lord has granted me the privilege, opportunity and desire to participate in this joint venture. While I bear the responsibility for the written words, all honor and glory goes to God.

For this collection of poems, I trust you find them enjoyable and perhaps some will even challenge your thinking.

God is the poet,
I am the recording secretary.

R. A. Gilmore

Foreword

*The steadfast love of the Lord never ceases,
his mercies never come to an end;
they are new every morning;
great is your faithfulness.*
(Lamentations 3:22-23, NRSV)

Brother Dick Gilmore and I met in 2015 on
a trip to India to visit the Sat Tal Christian
Ashram. I was able to travel with Brother
Dick in 2017 when we returned to the
beautiful countryside of Sat Tal. It was
common on those days at Sat Tal to find
Dick sitting at the round table on the
veranda with a notepad and pen at the ready,
as the Holy Spirit inspired those powerful
words that speak to the depth of many
people's hearts. I have sat at the same table
and not received the blessing of inspiration
but have experienced the blessing of the
fresh poetic expression shared with me
through Dick's most recent inspiration.

The common concept of blessings is
something good that happens in one's life
bringing joy, happiness, or contentment to

oneself. Yet, throughout the Scriptures and our experiences today, we recognize blessings include the presence of God in our most difficult and daunting times.

In Brother Dick's new book, we are invited to enter the emotions of *Blessings*. The blessing of rain, though coming from a dreary day, cleanses and renews the earth. The blessing of life shared with others brings about the pain of loss when a loved one passes from this life. The blessing of time is a gift to be treasured, even though we know the days may be numbered. The blessings that come when we least expect them and the blessings we miss when we don't see them in the present moment.

Each poem speaks into my heart, and one reminded me of a God-moment and blessing at the YMCA Hostel in Delhi, India. You will read in that poem where Brother Dick writes, "It may be through someone you've met." On the previous day, we met a young man named Mukesh who is a powerful evangelist, life-coach, and leader in India and throughout several places around the world. As I read the poem, my heart was filled with love and joy as I remembered the initial meeting and the growing relationship with Brother Mukesh. I was taken back to what some would say was a "chance meeting," but I see as a blessing from God.

As you read these marvelous and thought-provoking poems witness the reminder of God's blessings being abundant, overflowing, and extravagant. Note the reminder of the newness of God's blessings as the sun rises and sets on each day. Witness the movement through life stages of grief and celebration.

I am honored to write this Foreword for a mentor, friend, prayer partner, and encourager in my life. The wisdom Brother Dick has gained through experience and his close relationship with Jesus is well-established and proclaimed in his words. The blessing I have exceeds this book of poems to the deeper blessing of knowing this quiet, profound, and faithful follower of Jesus. I pray you will experience the great blessing of these God-inspired poems in your life.

Rev. Matthew Henson
Lead Evangelist/Executive Director
Living the Adventure Ministries

Executive Director
United Christian Ashrams International Ministry

Introduction

There are three sources examined for the definition of blessing:

- the internet
- Webster's Third International Dictionary
- Westminster Dictionary of the Bible.

There may be some similarities amongst the three, but there are distinct differences. Taking a definition from each source, we have the following:

- (internet) Words of a person who blesses.
- (Webster's) To consecrate or hallow by religious rite or word.
- (Westminster) Favors, advantages, conferred by God, and bringing pleasure or happiness.

Notice that the movement is from person to religion to God. To add to the question of definition, here are other definitions from each source.

- (internet): A special favor, mercy or benefit; a favor or gift bestowed by God, thereby bringing happiness; the invoking of God's favor upon a person; praise, devotion, worship especially grace before a meal; approval or good wishes.
- (Webster): to invoke divine care; an act of one who blesses; praise; worship.
- (Westminster): the invocation of God's favor upon a person; a present; a token of good will.

While each of these has the invoking of God's favor or divine care, the question arises of the source of the blessing. If I ask God to bless you, then it is clear that the blessing does not come from me, but from God. A blessing before a meal is the same situation, invoking God's favor to provide a blessing on the food. The blessing doesn't come from the one who is speaking, the blessing still comes from God.

There are several instances where the term blessing is used but with questionable intents and hence questionable source of the actual blessing. When a person sneezes, frequently someone will respond with "bless you" and think nothing of the saying. The saying is a shortened version of the original of "God bless you", invoking God to provide the blessing.

Another example is the southern expression of "bless your heart" which has been popularized and may actually be a derogatory statement. The question with this is, who is providing the blessing? Clearly if it is a derogatory statement, such a blessing is not from God.

Each of the poems in this book is invoking God to provide a blessing. God is a valuable source for providing blessings and His blessings store has an unlimited supply. One must bear in mind the fact that we may request God to bless, but the actual blessing will be at God's discretion.

One curious thing is when someone makes the statement "you have been such a blessing". In the process of serving God and ministering to His people, one may be providing comfort and assistance and the recipient perceives it as a blessing. The one doing the ministry is acting as an agent of God and at God's direction. The recipient has the sense of blessing, but the reality is the actual blessing is not from human agency but from a divine agency.

There are many poems in the book that share the same title. The title is not an item of concern, it is the content of each poem that matters. The poems are about various aspects of life or life experiences. Each of the poems titled "New Day" is about a different facet of the new day.

As you read these poems, let the poems open new vistas for you. Let them expand your horizons and draw you into a closer and deeper relationship with God.

God's Blessing

The many callings of the birds
Reverberate across the vales.
The sun has crested the high peaks,
The golden beams kiss hills and dales.

The breeze is still asleep in bed,
The coolness from the night hangs on.
The soul is quickened by the Lord
The calmness of God's new dawn.

Awake my spirit, greet the day,
Bask in this wonderful blessing
That God has graciously bestowed
So Him we can be confessing.

(Written while sitting on the porch of the
Mid Lakes at Sat Tal, India)

Blessings

A sweet peaceful balm laves the heart,
A peace that only God can give.
His loving arms embrace the soul
Making moments precious to live.

As the sun slips down in the west
It casts long shadows o'er the land.
Shadows depict God's growing love
That evermore it will expand.

How gracious is our loving God
Who gives special moments of bliss.
The blessings still He has in store
Are times that you don't want to miss.

(Written at the home of Marilyn and Tom Dumm
in Mayville, NY)

Blessings

The clouds have gathered in the sky.
They grew dark and began to cry.
God dispersed His washing machine
That His creation would be clean.

The aroma of rain-washed air,
As a sweet and refreshing flair,
Tickles the nose, lifts spirits high,
Eliciting a joyous sigh.

God's graciousness is on display
As He's sending His love our way.
God surprises at ev'ry turn,
For God's blessings we ever yearn.

Blessings

The sun crested horizon's brim,
Laving all with its golden rays.
The flowers respond to the touch,
And open with a yawning gaze.

We hear the chirping of the birds
And watch them hopping all around.
They rejoice to their creator
With praises that are heaven bound.

God's there to greet us each new morn,
To encourage us on our way.
His blessings banquet has been set;
His blessings are new ev'ry day.

Blessings

God has ushered in a new day
And His wonders are on display.
The orange orb has breached the rim
And the darkness is growing dim.

God puts right people on our way,
From them such helpful words they say.
Blessings abundantly do flow,
Making our heart and spirit glow.

God provides things to fall in place
And then our projects He does grace.
God's love laves ev'ry thing we do,
May our life let God's love shine through.

Blessings

God's Holy Spirit moves about
Dispensing blessings ev'ry day.
You never know just when or where
A blessing will be sent your way.

Always remain in God's good care,
Safely ensconced within His will.
New blessings will be ever poured
And each will bring a special thrill.

From God's abundant blessing store
Great gracious gifts do ever flow.
Be sure that when yours does arrive
Your gratitude to God does show.

(Written while flying
from Tucson, AZ to Atlanta, GA)

Blessings

Blessings come, often over flow,
Help is there, e'en when we don't know.
We accept, continue our days
As if these are usual ways.

We rarely pause, consider how
Things are happening in the now.
God is working behind the scenes
His will to do and with His means.

As we accept God's wondrous grace
There is a challenge that we face.
We must give thanks to God above
For His showers of gracious love.

Blessings

The breeze has now become a wind.
The trees their obeisance do pay.
The wind has brought along a friend,
A welcome cooling of the day.

Sometimes the wind is just a tease
To whet our appetite for cool.
We graciously accept the taste.
O'er such a change we almost drool.

Each change's an implement from God,
A blessing only He can pour.
He knows quite well just what we need
From His sweet blessing repertoire.

(Written while sitting on the porch of
the Mid Lakes at Sat Tal, India)

Blessings

Blessings do come and blessings go,
We never know which way they flow.
A simple gesture or a word
May bring a blessing when it's heard.

You speak a kind word on this day
And a blessing it does portray.
For us kind words may be routine,
For hearers a blessing they glean.

Sometimes a smile our face has pricked
And a blessing it does inflict.
What ere we do and what we say
May be God's blessing on this day.

Blessings

No party would be held today,
No surprise cards along the way.
No special dinner for tonight,
No gift that's wrapped and ribboned tight.

No fancy dessert to behold,
No special words would now be told.
For her the phone just didn't ring,
And that old song we did not sing.

Gentle sweet words were voiced to me
By many friends and family.
Fervent prayers were lifted above;
God poured out blessings and His love.

(This would have been
my wife Janine's 76th birthday)

Blessings

When we're not looking, blessings come.
God's blessings are new ev'ry day.
Though undeserving as we are
God's blessings still do come our way.

Give thanks to God for blessings sure.
Give thanks to God that He does care.
Let thanks to God be raised on high
As part of our daily prayer.

We take God's blessings as our due,
Complain when they're not as our way.
The Giver loves us ever much;
E'en calls us when we go astray.

Blessings Anew

Once more God's blessings arrive new
As harbingers of a fresh day.
Adorned with jewels of God's love
On His creation they do splay.

Bundles of blessings bounce about
Casting God's caresses with care,
Dancing on sunbeams and the breeze,
Exalting God, His love to share.

Fronds and boughs all frolic with glee,
Gracious obeisance they do pay,
Honoring God, their creator,
In their inimitable way.

(Written while visiting Marilyn and Tom Dumm in
Mayville, NY)

Blessings

Abundant blessings God does pour
On His people ev'ry moment.
His storehouse is never empty.
Blessings are given, never lent.

Blessings to us are numberless
And yet to count them we should try.
We very quickly would discern
They're more than the stars in the sky.

None of God's blessings we can earn.
He provides them and they are free.
Because of God's great love for us,
He blesses extravagantly.

Blessings

God's blessings come in many ways,
Often it will be a surprise.
They come when you least expect it
E'en though it's right before your eyes.

It may be a quite large event.
It may be something very small.
It may be through someone you've met.
It may be from God's direct call.

Is your spirit set to receive
And is your heart in the right place?
God's blessings store's always open
And it is you God wants to grace.

(Written at the New Delhi YMCA
Tourist Hostel, India)

Blessings

Abundant blessings are in store
To be dispensed throughout this day.
God's angels will be on the prowl
To see who's following God's way.

God's Spirit roams hither and yon
Giving blessings as He does see.
Those blessings bring much joy and hope
As they are giv'n to you and me.

Blessings draw us closer to God
And thanks to Him we do bestow.
Each blessing enhances our life
And to the Christ closer we grow.

(Written at Tulip Grove Baptist Church,
Old Hickory, TN)

Blessings

Dew-kissed grass glistens in the sun,
Golden rays long shadows do cast.
A gentle breeze kisses the face.
It's God's idyllic scene so vast.

As the earth turns, shadows do shrink,
Golden rays become more intense.
The glassy dew yields to the rays
And hides itself in its defense.

God's creative work continues,
His handiwork is on display.
God's blessings on us overflow
As we embark on this new day.

Blessings

The new morning has awakened,
Its brightness spreads across the land.
God has blessed His new creation
And that blessing is very grand.

Azure has spread its canopy
And embraces the golden rays.
It is a new inspiration,
A gift from the Ancient of Days.

Awake oh spirit, ope' your eyes.
Bask in the blessings this day brings.
Breathe deeply of this new off'ring
Of which the angelic choir sings.

(Written at Covenant Presbyterian Church,
Nashville, TN)

Blessings

The day began so dark and drear
With thick black clouds hanging so low.
With gusty winds the clouds did cry
As a torrential rain did flow.

Persistent were the weeping ones
As through the day their tears did show.
The pesky clouds did stay so long
And light was just a hazy glow.

God does provide His cleansing scheme
As the earth and air He does lave.
The aftermath will smell so sweet,
Another blessing that God gave.

(Written while sitting in the lobby of
the choir room at Covenant Presbyterian Church,
Nashville, TN)

Blessings

God has provided a new day.
His wondrous love is on display.
With the golden beams of the sun
His gracious blessings have begun.

There is so much He has in store
That on us He will gently pour.
Whatever we have planned to do
His blessings will still follow through.

Busyness may consume our day
Yet God's love will still hold full sway.
Blessings will still be ev'rywhere
Because our God does truly care.

(Written while sitting in the waiting area
of the Vanderbilt Medical Center)

Blessings

We have been graced with a new year,
There are many blessings in store.
Blessings will come as God directs
And as the Spirit does outpour.

Hearts should be opened, well prepared
To receive what God does supply.
Blessings offered but not accepted
Back to the sender they will fly.

God's blessings do adorn our life
And do help us to rightly live.
As these blessings do freely flow
To God, many thanks we should give.

(Written at Tulip Grove Baptist Church,
Old Hickory, TN)

God's Blessings Tide

The morning had made its debut,
God had dispatched His wake-up call.
The wind was slow to greet the day,
Only a breeze it could install.

Those morning rays did make a show
By dancing on the silver threads
Of cobwebs that were spun at night
Dangling between the deck chair heads.

The humming birds now make their rounds
As the blossoms have opened wide.
These creatures of God do respond
By riding on His blessings tide.

(Written while visiting Marilyn and Tom Dumm
in Mayville, NY)

God's Blessings

O Lord, Your blessings do abound
When we're up high or on the ground.
Even if we're under the sea
Your blessings flow so great and free.

When we're perplexed and under fire
Your blessings flow and us inspire.
When we are steeped in our sorrow
Blessings help us reach tomorrow.

When all is well and going fine
It's due to Your blessings divine.
When we're asleep throughout the night
Your blessings keep us from all fright.

When we're alone You bless us still,
Our empty hearts You then do fill.
Lord, where in this world would we be
Without blessings and love from Thee?

(Written while flying from Minneapolis,
MN to San Diego, CA)

God's Blessings

God has spawned another new day
Bathed with the sun's warm golden ray.
Through the stained glass those beams do
   shine
Casting images so divine.

Unique patterns those beams display
Adorned with a color array.
As the sun continues its rise
Patterns provide a quaint surprise.

God's wondrous schemes reach far and wide
Pouring out blessings like a tide.
God's artistry is in plain view
As He blesses both me and you.

(Written as Covenant Presbyterian Church,
Nashville, TN)

God's Blessings

I am so weak but God is strong,
I'm where He wants me to belong.
He is my strength and He's my shield,
Only to Him my soul does yield.

Though I have aches and I have pain
Through all this God's love does sustain.
On life's path that does turn and wind
Great solace in Him I do find.

As life's vagaries ebb and flow
Blessings God continues to show.
Although I'm destined to face death
I'll still praise God through my last breath.

God's Blessings

Weather may be damp and dreary
And a bone-chilling wind may blow,
Through it all you are running late,
Keep alert, God's blessings still flow.

It seems ev'rything's gone awry,
The day just didn't start out right.
Troubles appear, beset each step,
E'en through this God's blessings are bright.

What ere your perspective might be
For activities of the day,
Keep heart and mind focused on God
And God's blessings will come your way.

(Written at the Donelson-Hermitage YMCA)

Blessings

God's Spirit on earth does patrol
Seeking hearts under God's control,
Hearts that ever God do extol,
Hearts that ere seek God as their goal.

The Spirit looks where hearts abide,
Those hearts that keep Christ at their side,
Those hearts that on God's grace they ride,
Those hearts where only God is guide.

The Spirit seeks hearts that are true
To Christ's leadings in all they do,
Hearts where Christ's love ever shines
  through,
There the Spirit blessings imbue.

(Written at the Donelson-Hermitage YMCA)

www.ingramcontent.com/pod-product-compliance
Lightning Source LLC
Chambersburg PA
CBHW061758040426
42447CB00011B/2355